why things burn

POEMS BY
DAPHNE GOTTLIEB

Why Things Burn

Daphne Gottlieb

Soft Skull Press
2001

Why Things Burn
ISBN: 1-887128-65-4
copyright 2001, Daphne Gottlieb

The author wishes to thank Nick Mamatas, Sander Hicks and Soft Skull;
Thea Hillman, Lauren Wheeler, the Ignition Poets and the E-Is; the Mills
poets, Jackie Graves and Dani Montgomery; the performance poetry com-
munity; everyone who has given up their ears, their confidences or their floor
space to help; my friends and family, for absolutely everything, especially
their faith; and, most of all, Miriam Kronberg.

Thanks to the following publications, where some of these poems appear in
slighty different forms: *The Exquisite Corpse, Fengi.com,The Labyrinth,*
nakedpoetry.com, Nerve.com, Poetry Slam! The Competitive Art of
Performance Poetry (Manic D Press), *Real Poetik, The San Francisco Bay*
Guardian, (sic) vice and verse, Swallow Your Pride, Urban Spaghetti, The
Walrus, the Better Living Through Amplification festival chapbook, and the
chapbooks *Choke, Clutch, Throttle,* and *You Break It, You Bought It.*

Editorial: Nick Mamatas
Design: David Janik
Cover Art: Kim Stringfellow
Author Photograph: Kari Holmquist

You can order this book and other great Soft Skull Press titles
at a big discount from *www.softskull.com.*

Distributed to the book trade by PGW
1 800 788 3123 *www.pgw.com*

SOFT SKULL PRESS, INC.
98 Suffolk Street no. 3A
New York, NY 10002

TABLE OF CONTENTS

a girl never knows when she's gonna need to soak up some blood

lather, rinse and revolution

"fire is beautiful
and we know that if we get
too close it will kill us
but what does that matter
it is better to be happy
for a moment
and be burned up with beautiful
than to live a long time
and be bored all the while..."

—don marquis,
from *archy and mehitabel,*
"the lesson of the moth"

a

girl

never

knows

when

she's

gonna

need

to

soak

up

some

blood

mastering the art of poetry

(with thanks to Dossie Easton;
some text kidnapped from her manual, *The Topping Book*)

make sure you have everything
you will need
on hand:

pen   paper   or computer keyboard
dictionary   thesaurus   scissors (surgical)
tape   first-aid kit   plastic wrap
feathers   candles   clothespins
gag   rope   handcuffs
an assortment of whips
from fat thudding floggers
to bitey braided cats
maybe a wooden paddle
rubbing alcohol
piercing sharps
scalpel
a cane or two
and a riding crop.

got everything?
good.

negotiate,
negotiate,
negotiate.

if you want your poem to beg or struggle,
make that clear.
listen to your poem's desires
and get ready

to be powerful and terrible.
your poem is quivering in front of you
and your iron will
as it kisses the collar you hold.

{3

begin.

start
slowly.

gradually.

maybe a little stroking, teasing pinches, a few
words chosen
carefully
go a long way.

now escalate.
if you've startest with your
gentlest, sweetest metaphor,
it's time to build up to something a little
harder.

feel it? your poem opening up, reeling,
writhing, relinquishing control?
good.

take it right to the edge of what it can stand
then back off
then right to the edge
and back off again
up to a farther edge
as your poem swells
with the marks you leave on its skin

one thank you master
two thank you master
three thank you master

as you push it, drag it, hold it down
raise it up

THANK YOU MASTER

tell your poem
"you're about to get a verb you'll never forget, you little slut."

tell your poem,
"I want to hear you scream."

tell your poem
"you only get forty more words, you greedy bitch!"
and when it has taken all it can bear

hold that precious poem close
show it how much it has pleased you
and rest. give it your name
and kiss it
goodnight.

She's
kinky,

and she's
given up dating.

She's fallen in love and
given up

dating and
her whips

as youthful
foolishness.

Her chaps are gathering dust in the closet
and her corset sits like an empty saddle

after the horse has left or run
away, or been flogged to death.

*He's not like
the others.*

*He's a very special
man,* she says.

*I'm glad he makes you
so happy,* I tell her.

He treats me so well,
she says.

The weekend I visited,
he was hunting deer

with his father.
It's okay, she tells me.

He eats what he kills.
Okay.

It's like that sometimes,
I guess.

Maybe something is only yours
when you can do as you please with it

since now, she has
no need

for the ridiculous literal
liturgy of S&M—

no more dress-up.
No make-believe.

All the black leather
she needs

is the E-Z boy recliner
where her love is parked

with one of his hands wrapped around a remote,
the other, a bottle of beer.

She's right. It's kinky,
the way he doesn't look away

from the TV,
as her head bobs

in his lap
like a fisherman's float

on a nature program,
hectic

with the pace
his breath sets.

His crotch swells
under her mouth's

prowess. He's such
a sweetheart

he waits
until the

commercials
to come.

attacquette

(THE GRACIOUS HOSTESS DRESSES FOR COMPANY)

i)   wearing a walkman can impede hearing
ii)   do not wear clothing so tight as to constrict movement
iii)   do not wear attire that you can not run in
iv)   interlace your keys between your fingers

(THE POLITE LADY KNOWS HOW TO GREET HER GUESTS)

v)   the buddy system
vi)   do not yell for help
vii)   do not struggle
viii) whatever you did is correct

                    i shouldn't have   i didn't mean
ix)   the important thing is to stay alive

                    get away
x)   do not allow yourself to be moved to a second location   {9

                    or i'll scream

(THE CHARMING HOMEMAKER KNOWS HOW TO MAKE CONVERSATION)

xi)   do not yell

                    people are expecting me
xii)   do not yell for help

                    don't do this
xiii) do not yell *help* yell *fire*

                    please
xiv)   struggle and fight to elude the aggressor
xv)   whatever you did to survive was the right thing

                    *do not wear attire so tight as to constrict
                    movement*
xvi)   struggle may encourage an aggressor

(ASKING GUESTS ABOUT THEMSELVES IS A SURE WAY TO WIN FRIENDS)

xvii) eyes

                why are you doing this?

xviii) knees

                                   please leave me alone

xix) groin

                                        can't i just go home

xx)   throat

                                                if i never tell anybody?

(HAVE AN ENCHANTING BUFFET FOR A LIGHT LATE SUPPER)

xxi) knife

                eyes

xxii) gun

                        knees

xxiii) pepper spray

                               groin

xxiv) brass knuckles

                                    throat

xxv) any weapon you carry can be used against you

(THANK GUESTS FOR THEIR COMPANY)

10}

xxvi) 9-1-1

(REMEMBER: A STRANGER IS A FRIEND YOU HAVEN'T MET YET!)

xxvii) don't yell *help* yell   *fire*

                                          fire

                          fire

We stood on tiptoes for you, Barbie,
hoping it was not our faces
that would freeze (as our mothers
warned) but our feet. We scrolled them
into sea shells until they cramped that way
and we waited to grow.

We wanted your life: always on your way to somewhere
golden and glamorous: the beach, a party—
you were always
ready to go; your make-up
was always perfect and even your home
was a dream house
and we wanted your
life but you
shared ours.

You perfected what we did not yet have words for:
virgin, whore and complex.
You were built for longing
but not for need. You
are an acetate seashell locked
tight. We ripped your legs off,
like diners at a cracked crab feast, but found nothing
to sate our early appetites. We aspired to be whole
just like you. We drew down each others' pants
just to be sure but finding no easy fix, we inked
a small slit on you instead and still
you were perfect
and oh we wanted to
be like you since you could be anything:
doctor, fashion model, ballerina, mini-mart
clerk, rock star. You could even be african-
american and latina. We wanted your life but
you shared ours and everyone—oh! everyone
loved you. We loved
you for being like us: our
open eyes stared

together
at our door
at night
we waited
together
we held dry, cold hands
in the dark—
you showed us
how long
to hold our breath for
and how
still to stay
but Barbie:

you bested
us again. You never
bruised. You
never cried out.
And when morning came,
there was almost always
a new dress for you
waiting
at breakfast.

death drive
(a transfession)

*"We are rebels because those who govern us, often—blindly, no doubt—
betray us."*
            —Nance O'Neill, lover of Lizzie Borden

18/19/20XX

Dear Mother/Daughter/Darling/God/Guns/To Whom it may Concern,

I'm sorry it's been so long since I've written.
I'm sorry I've been out of touch.
I'm sorry for what I did.
You'll never hear from me again.
There are a few things I wanted to tell you.
They're going to kill me.
This is all your fault.

You wanted to know the truth:
It happened on the hottest day of the year
          /when I was fifteen
          /because I was pregnant
          /in the shipyards. They called me "seagull" because

I flocked around the sailors
I had food poisoning
I ran away from juvie
I crawled into my stepfather's lap
I just wanted him to love me
I pretended I was asking for directions
I asked for the head of John the Baptist
I shoved the girl into the car
I thought we were going to get married, but

he sent me this letter
he touched me when I was fifteen
he was the man of my dreams
he touched my son
he said marry a nice guy
he said act like a nice girl

{13

he had money
he gave me junk
he killed himself by pointing the gun between his legs and shooting
he was shooting up
he liked to fuck virgins up the ass
he wanted my sister
he wanted to videotape it
he said he'd marry me if I didn't have kids
he said he'd kill me if I didn't—
he'd steal my stash
                    —if I didn't do it

so I shot him in /the sitting room/the court room/the church parking lot/the hot
tub/the shipyard with
              an ax/tranquilizers/kerosene/
                    with no other choice/with all my strength/with all his
                         money/with/love
they were asleep in the back of the car
they were waiting for me
they found me not guilty
they found the videotapes
they sentenced me to life
they were going to kill my baby
they found him not guilty
they deserved it
they found me guilty
they found him in the bullrushes
they ripped open my mouth, my cunt
they were sure I did it but

                    there was no blood on my clothes
                    there was no future for them, but maybe for me
                    there was a river nearby
                    there was blood everywhere
                    there was the ax in the basement
                    there was the sound of the car slipping into the water
                         /into my vein
                         /into unconsciousness
                         /into hotels with sailors and ripping
                         /off their wallets
                              /their clothes
                              /my body

I left home
I left fingerprints
I left the headlights on
      /the door unlocked
      /the baby at
      /the river bank
I lit the match and ran out
I said a black man stole my car
I said, "His head on a platter"
I crawled into his lap
I was sure no one would get hurt
I wanted his money
I wanted him to pay
I put the car in neutral and pushed
I watched it sink

I burned my dress
I never confessed
I'll get you for this
I pray God forgives me
I'd do it all again
I know God knows the/guns/God
I know God knows the truth:

I settled down
I took a lover
I took /God/guns
I did it for him
I'm doing life
I'd do it again if I had the/God/guns
I'd shoot him again if I had the chance—

You wanted to know the truth.
Here it is:

I got blood all over the seat but kept driving/my blood stuck me to the seat
and I kept driving/bloody/driven across the border/here now the signs say
God/Guns/God/Guns/God at 50 miles per hour/the signs/say
God/Guns/God/at 60 miles per hour the signs/say God/Guns/when I go/I
go fast/fast enough I can make them/the signs/the blood/I make them/say
it/fast/I just say/

                          Go—

nature and fate*

If ever man was loved
by wife, then thee;
               he had his hand on the
               inside of my thigh
                              with no effect on
                              controlling what
                              happened

As I grew up to be about
14 or 15, I found my
heart more carnal.
               He said, "Good girls
               never tell"
                              when aversive stimulus
                              was repeated over and
                              over again

the Lord laid His hand
16}   sore upon me and smote
me
               and you don't call police
               on him. You just don't
               call the police. He
               already told me 'Don't
               call the police on me
               'cause I will kill you"
                              and the motivation to
                              respond would be
                              lessened. The response to
                              stimulus would
                              disappear completely.

on my death bed
               he was going to kill me
                              and disappear completely
I have no sooner felt my
heart out of order, but I
have expected correction
for it

*Texts are culled from Anne Bradstreet's poetry and prose,
accounts by battered women, and Seligman's research on
learned helplessness.

and, uh, he was upset
because I couldn't get
him the money to buy
drugs. It was my ass
when I couldn't get him
the money

        to disappear completely

before I was afflicted,
but now I keep Thy
statutes

    I couldn't get him the
    money

        to put dogs in cages

I went astray

    at 4 or 5 in the morning.
    He would wake me up
    by hitting me

        and administered
        electrical shocks at
        random. At varied
        intervals,

                                    {17

I have been in darkness
and seen no light

    since he worked nights

        no matter what response
        these dogs made to
        control the shocks, it did
        not help

sickness, weakness, pain,
 doubts and fears

    slapping, yelling and hitting

        many of the dogs.
        Various voluntary
        movements were made
        to escape the shocks.

I have oft thought if the
Lord would but lift up
the light of His
countenance upon me,

    he would say, "Her eyes
    are like that because she
    wanted green ones so I

gave her black ones"

        since none of their
        movements could halt
        the shocks, the dogs
        ceased all further
        activity

it would be but light to
me

    when he said he was
    sorry

        and the dogs accepted the
        shocks

although He ground me
to powder

    he said he was sorry

        and became passive, sub-
        missive, and compliant

it would be but light to
me

    when he said, "you're a
    good girl, nothing will
    happen to you"

        when they could have
        escaped. The doors to
        the cages were open.

I can now say... if I
perish, I perish.

    It's only a power greater
    than me that keeps me
    alive

        and the dogs accepted
        the shocks

see what ways of
wickedness are in me

    no one believed me

        and the dogs accepted
        the shocks

*incubus/succubus**

Psyche continued her wanderings.   Every daughter presumes parents.

I want to start today with the image of the Black Widow.   He fucks her.
Then she bites his head off.   Every story ends the same, in death, and
every story happens here.   A spider is not a woman.   A map is not
a place.

Aileen: I used to live in an old junked car in the woods, hitchhiked
        everywhere, got raped, oh, maybe 10 or 12 times.

His soul fluttered to rest in the kingdom of God.   There are no killers
here: 16th and South Van Ness   14th and Duboce   15th and Albion
23rd and San Jose   22nd and Fair Lawn   19th and Lexington   :no
women and no lives   *That is*   just words   *not the scene of writing*
all I have is anecdotal evidence   *where the author's desire is staged.*
all I can do is bear witness.   *You are the only one who ever listened*

24th and Mission   *The confrontation with the necessity of being saved*
she sold her mouth for money   *from such pathology*   she could not
use it to talk her way out   *the confrontation*   her body opened
with the very real risks of 'nymphomania' and 'erotomania'.   27 bloody
mouths   gasping   gaping   she spread her legs for money and that's
how they found her   *I saw her*   (all I can do is bear witness)
propped up against the dumpster   behind Walgreen's   *"Girls look so*
old nowadays."

The equator swam behind tears.   None of you can prevent this.

Mrs. America: I saw her on all of those shows.

---

*Italics indicate textual intercourse with Virginia Woolf,
Jane Gallop, the Theory Girls,an anthology of love stories
and others.

18th and Valencia   she had no shoes and her bedroll had been stolen
I used to look at the pictures and think *'After I'm dead, they won't even
know what I look like—* some sort of wire   made her throat smile
—they won't even have a picture of me.' all that was left behind was
a shrine

Psyche continued her wanderings. She wandered through many lands
the flowers died   and someone stole   the candles   *searching for Eros*

Only the streets still have names   17th and Guerrero   *I know*   15
steps in the staircase   *I know women*   she landed face down   grew
a puddle of urine and blood   she   *I know women have been
victimized*   on concrete   face down   drowned   *but it is absolutely
essential that we stop*   it was days   before she was found   *thinking
of ourselves as victims*

20}

no names   *I want to start today with the image of the Black Widow.*
Does language describe or conjure   kill   save   abandon   *She held
on until her strength gave out*   this trap waiting for us   *we stop
thinking of ourselves as victims*   a map is not a place   *Then she let
go and fell to the ground, exhausted.*   does it happen every time?   27
gaping mouths   the flowers died   face down   *exhausted*   None of
you could stop   this   every   story

*Aileen: You are the only one, the only one who ever listened to me.
       I can die happy in that knowledge.*

I want to start   describe   conjure   bear witness   it is absolutely
essential

Mrs. America:

i'm
suffering from
job burnout
today.
the
pay
is shitty, the
hours are unending
and i'm overworked since
these days every time i walk down
the street there's a woman being hurt. later,
these women somehow get directions and show
up in my head, ringing the buzzer, crawling through
the window when i don't answer and waiting in line
to be written into a poem, for words to give them impermeable,
permanent bodies. right now, there are too many to count, hundreds,
maybe even thousands, shuffling their feet, waiting in line, their hands
knotting and unknotting in their laps, nursing their children, blowing
their noses, waiting. why didn't i take that job writing about wild
strawberries and childhood like my mother wanted? there is another
woman here, too, bound to me by genetics and memory. in another
country, she hunts killers in women's blood and writes to me in light:
after the diagnosis, what then? then the word neither of us can say. from
different sides of the globe, we dig at the tight knots of history until
our hands are raw and still we cannot make *unkill* a word and all the
women we cannot save. there is always work. the women in my head
are growing restless, pulling at the crime scenes of their bodies,
wrestling with the police line tape that binds them together like
memory or genetics. i stick my fingers in my mouth and blow, a whistle
so loud it is heard on pages five continents away. their searchlight eyes
widen as i tell them: ladies, i have had enough. today, we're going to
do it differently. i'll tell you what. grab a beer from the fridge. turn on
the radio too loud, open the window and dance. inflate the body bags
into balloons and set them free into the sky. put on a party hat.
remember how to laugh until your throat hurts. tell me a story that
ends "and they lived happily ever after" because this is your poem and
it's a party and nothing bad will happen to you here. when everything
else has fallen apart, this will still stand; this is your memorial, your
sanctuary, your legacy. come on in.
stay forever.
welcome.

Wrapping and wrapping around
the steel-and-rubber car wheel,

Isadora Duncan's scarf
was a noose, a love letter

of how beauty kills. In the newspaper
I read that an average

woman applies at least
10 carcinogenic

products to her body
in the morning before she leaves

for work, that other
slow death. It doesn't matter.

Our irradiated food
preserves us from the inside

and the traffic makes fossils
of our skin. We are carbon-

dating at the end
of the century, making sure

there's a good looking corpse to leave
and who's looking? And who's good?

Lipstick used to have names like
Passion Pink, Love's Blush or Sin

Red. Now it's Media, Cult,
Diva, Rebel, War, Carnal,

Metal, Fetish, Jet, Bruise,
Roach, Frostbite, Vamp; Photo-

graphs will tell us that beauty
is only skin deep, but we just

want to be skinny, not deep—
we just want to halt traffic,

mouths red as stop lights, our scarves
arranged around our throats and we

put the hammer to the floor.
We are in the driver's seat.

We look so good these days
we're just too happy to hear

that in the mortuary
they use our brand of make-up.

X-Originating-IP: [000.00.00.00]
From: "badgirl" <badgirl@hotmail.xxx>
To: letters@only18.com
Subject: Wow!
MIME-Version: 1.0
Date: Thu, 03 Dec 1999 20:07:42 PST

Dear Only18,

I've never read a magazine like yours before, but after today I just had to write to you! I never knew that there was a magazine about girls just like me!

I was walking home from my baby-sitting job and I was kind of bored. I mean, you know how it can be, right? I mean, just school and baby-sitting and going to the mall on weekends and a party now and then.

24} Today, everything changed, though. I was walking down the street and this guy was leaning against his car. I've never thought of older men as sexy until I saw him. He had sexy, silver hair and a great smile. He tipped his head toward his car and opened the door, and I don't know what got into me—I just hopped in! It was just like he'd been waiting for me!

He closed the car door on my side and walked around the car. He slid in and looked at me. "Well," he said, "we'd better get you buckled in." His hands slid up by my shoulder and pulled the belt across my chest. My nipples strained against my sweater as his hands ran across me. I could feel myself getting wet as he pulled my scrunchie out of my hair. He gathered my hands in one of his and wrapped my wrists together in it. He pushed my hands between my legs and I moaned from the pressure against the seam of my jeans. "Now you're nice and safe," he said, and started the car.

"Didn't your mother ever tell you not to talk to strangers?" he asked. "Bad things could happen." He ran his hand down my face and fucked my mouth with his fingers—no matter how hard and deep I sucked, there was always more! I sucked until his hand filled my mouth. Just when I thought he'd rip my mouth apart or I'd pass out from not breathing, he pulled his hand away and started the car.

I could feel the engine throbbing like it was right between my legs—even though it was winter, we didn't need the heater! He drove fast but I kept wishing he'd drive faster—get us wherever we were going sooner. Every time he stopped the car, my hands pushed against my wet pussy through my jeans, making me gasp. And he'd just laugh, but I could tell he was getting hot, too. I could see his big, hard cock was ready for action through his khakis.

We pulled into his house on the outside of town. He stopped the engine and I couldn't wait!!! He helped me out of the car, and walked me up his steps into his house. It was dark except for the glow of his computer screen—linked to only18.com—and the TV lighting up the room with an "Only 18" video—the girl was like me! She had the same color hair, anyway. But she was soooo sexy—she was lying on a bed, stroking her soft, sweet pussy, and I could tell she was just as wet as I was! I wanted to hear what she was saying, but the sound was all the way down. I lay down in front of the TV and kicked my sneakers off.

"Messy, messy," he said. "Look at what a bad girl you are," he said. He slipped my sweater over my head and around my wrists. When he twisted my nipples through my bra, I thought I was going to die from the pleasure.

{25

I couldn't wait to get my mouth around his big, thick cock, but he was going to make me wait. He said "I know all about little girls. For one thing, little girls should be seen and not heard." He pulled a roll of duct tape and a knife out from a drawer in the TV stand. His strong hand held me off the floor by my hair as he wrapped the duct tape over my mouth, slicing it from the roll with his big knife, and kissing me through it. God, he was hot, teasing me like that. I wanted it, wanted all 8 inches of it and I'd never wanted anything like that before. He let go of me so suddenly I fell back to the floor, and he walked over to his laptop. "Little girls like bedtime stories, too," he said, "but you don't look sleepy yet." He pulled me to my knees as only a man can—he was letting me know all about being a woman—and set the laptop in front of me. "I'll tell you a story, and you can type it nmxfereu HLP
ME
TID UP
555XGT
SND HLP
KDNP KDNPKIDNAP
HES MKNGME WRT THS SND HLP 524 MAPL;;

oh honey honey I'm telling you—a woman's work is never
done. why that guy who gave me the once-over twice,
pumping his hands under his overcoat—
well, his eyes don't open so well
since I sprayed him in the face with my
Miss Lady Aerosol Pump Superhold Formula Hairspray

and then that guy who felt me up on the subway, well—
blame it on my Lady Eve Press-on Manicure Nails in Sin Red
and something about that kind of fruit, why
that adam's apple just fell right out
ripe and red into my hand

and that guy on the corner calling me everyday
with his *hey baby baby doncha wanna baby baby*
doncha wanna piece of me
and I said *yeah baby baby yeah I wanna piece of you*
and took off a one-inch slab of his tongue
with my Non-slip Grip Lady Schick

and oh those guys who tried to jump
me on the way home—oh don't you know
these things always end in tears
I was so sorry to lose my favorite pair of Foxy Lady
Five-inch Patent Leather Spike Heels—it's going
to be a while before I get over that one

but a girl's got to do what a girl's got to do
and don't even start me on what happened
the night that guy broke into my sanitary
pad—it took me hours to clean off my Curling
Iron, my Nail File, my Tweezers, my Just-For-Me
Sandal Toe Queen Size Control Tops are still hanging out to dry

and what with all the screaming
I'm lucky I didn't get caught red-
handed with my Pink Comfort-Tip
Scented Double-Barrel Super-Plus Sawed-

26}

Off Tampax but Thank God for
feminine protection.

A girl never knows when she's gonna need
to soak up some blood.

This is the part no one talks about:
How the goddamn translator
fucked everything up.

If she'd only kept her name,
not been Americanized,
she'd still be *Aschenputtel,*
a name like a whisper
or a kiss.

If her pals still called her "Assypuss,"
not "Cindy" or "Cinder" or even "Ella,"
maybe she would have had a shot at a real
man, maybe a plastic surgeon ass man
or a construction worker to jackhammer
into her for hours
or even just work her clit
now and then.

But no.
It had to be a prince
with a foot fetish—
the glossy stacks of *Leg World,*
Leg Show, Toe Girls,
under the bed,
Lloyd's of London's 12 billion dollar
insurance policy
on her feet.

And that fucking translator.
It was all his fault.
If he'd known *vair* was fur and not
verre, glass, she'd have a closet
with silky, sumptuous shoes of mink,
fox, maribou, seal,
and her feet would sink into them
like butter.

Instead, her shoes are the unforgiving ice
of hand-blown Sisley glass,
sea-sanded coke bottle glass, mirrored disco ball glass,
crazy-quilt stained glass.

Every night, the same thing.
The translator and her husband come
pouring sickly sweet champagne
for themselves, never her.
She doesn't care.
She sips at her whisky
and stares at the yellow ceiling
until it's over.

The prince sits nearby
as the translator slides the shoe
off her left foot, slowly,
slowly it caresses her left heel,
hushes slowly over the left arch,
and slithers away from her toes, slowly,
slowly.

Then the prince slobbering at her foot like a puppy dog,
a big, drooly one, making her shoe ring like a crystal wine glass
as his tongue runs laps around the open toe.

Her foot
down
the prince's
throat,
as deep as he
can get it
until her foot
cramps
and his eyes
water
and the spot
shines
on the front of his
pants.

The translator waits nearby
with a towel, creams, polish,
pumice stone, oils,
emery boards, and a fucking closet
full of glass slippers:
platforms, mules, slingbacks,
oxfords, wingtips, stilettos,
pumps. What the hell
is she supposed to do
with fifty pairs of glass
running shoes ferchrist'ssake?

He forbids her
to run, even walk—
corns, calluses, plantar's warts,
bunions, ringworm,
athlete's foot—

Her sisters had it right
the first time around,
slicing off their toes, their heels.
Let them have him.

She sharps the ax slowly,
slowly, with a lover's
caress.

There is $12 billion
in a Swiss bank account
and a wheelchair
waiting for her
in the Caymans.

No one will ever find her.
No one will be looking
for Assypuss.

She draws a red line
just above her ankles,
where the bones
are thinnest.
She tears her wedding dress

into white satin
bandages.

Soon she will grow new skin
on the end of her shins,
tender as baby
buttocks, translucent
as glass.

She can't wait.
She's ready. All she needs
is a little more sharpening
and a little more scotch.

We only get the superheroes
we can imagine, never
the ones we need.

*We don't need more
superheroes, just better ones,*
say the idealists.

Third-world Marxists say,
*If we build a superhero, she will be nothing
like Wonder Woman.*

*There is so much wrong
with Wonder Woman:
She is white when*

*most of the world isn't. She has a jet
which is a gas-guzzler, usurping resources
that might better serve the people.*

You're wrong, say the feminists.
*You're missing what is really wrong
with Wonder Woman, how her body*

*type is unsustainable
for most women and it is unhealthy
how she is put on display*

*in a see-thru jet, the Fredrick's of Hollywood
of air travel, a 360-degree glass ceiling
that moves as fast as she does*

*and another thing—no one makes
Aquaman run
in four-inch heels, and—*

Fighting crime is still fighting, say the pacifists. *No fighting.*
You are short-sighted, say the militants.
You are missing the point, say the post-colonialists.

Oh yeah? say the Promise Keepers.
    A woman's place is—
Who let YOU in? ask the lesbian separatists.

It comes to blows quickly, over a question
of who is the most wrong
and everyone has forgotten altogether

about Wonder Woman,
who has slipped out
through the back

of the discussion,
as invisible
as her jet.

How to save the world this time?
She tosses her bullet-deflecting bracelets
and her golden lasso

into the trash
and leaves her superheadband
perched on top, shining dully.

She is too tired.
Let them damn well fight
their own damned crime.

what mama bear said

It was my son's screaming
that made me come running.

My claws raking the sky,
I roared in,
saw little white panties
flit out his window,
then small, pale legs,
shiny black shoes.

It hadn't been a wild animal
at all, the missing
porridge, the broken
chair, the long slithery hairs,
that smell.

How could we call the cops?
A house of bears
looks like game
to men with guns.

My son screams in his sleep now,
and I roar in,
claws raking the sky.
I quiet him as best I can.

Every night he tells me
how tendrils of blonde hair
curl from his bed—snaking out,
gagging his mouth,
blinding his eyes—
and devour everything
that was once his.

I lullaby his thick bear head
back under sleep
whisper to him,
It was just a dream.

His heavy head
under my paw,
I watch the window,
stay awake,
since I,
I know better.

speaking siamese in england

(for conjoined twins born August 2000)

When they talk to us   from the left,
they call us
Mary.
From the right,   they call us
Jodie.
We have yet to open   our four eyes.
We tear at our skin   with our two balled fists.

           We   am a British girls,
unagreeable in your tongue, unsayable in the Queen's English.
It is like this:
When the head on our left is hungry,
the head on our right   screams.

Not Jodie on the left and Mary on the right—
do you name each of your hands?—
but MaryJodie   or   JodieMary

The doctors,   eager explorers
on the newest America of our body
claim us   in parts:
Mary's lung.   Jodie's heart.
They plant their flags and sharpen their knives.
Mary must die, they say, to save Jodie.

Brain damaged,   they say of Mary,
as if she is not me   as if we are not she
as if we are not us.
But if I am Jodie,   and I am our heart
and one lung,   why not our brain as well?
Families, we've heard, should support each other.

There are two beats to every pulse.

We come from   a monstrous love
from two people   so rapt

<pre>
        in sweat,   in joy
        two arms,   one head
        could not   hold it all.
    There is never   much love.

This is how your world treats holy:

                               if God spoke through us,
                               you would replace his words
                               with thorazine, halidol;

        if he was calling us home,
        you would pump our husk
            with blood or air
    and the doctors would shout

            IT'S A MIRACLE! It's
                    alive
    We will not be   your miracle.
                    We
                    will
                    not
        be cleaved   down our center,
    the gash of God's mouth   stitched shut.
    We would rather die   than grow up like a girl,
a walking grave in our side,   some stunted topiary
            of   your   success.

        We are holy,   too whole
            for   your   world.
            She   is   my sister
            is me   is us:
        JodieMary   MaryJodie,
        MoanieJary,   Jamaramodie.
    We wrap my arms   around ourself
        and I will not   let us
                    go.
</pre>

{37

Sure, you could probably say it's my fault. You could say it's because of the cigarettes and the alcohol, but the doctors don't. Believe me, I've been second-guessing them all along. Ever since they told me to take lots of baths to stop the spasms.

That's what the doctors said. It was a bad pregnancy, a back pregnancy, whatever that is. It hurt like a motherfucker, and it meant I spent five months of my life lying down, taking baths, renting movies, reading magazines, when all I wanted was to be back to my life.

His dad was on the swim team. That's what I think caused it.

That, and because I saw "The Little Mermaid" when I was pregnant. I only saw it once, not over and over, but maybe once was enough.

It's funny how I can call him a dad when all he did was call the lord's name in vain and use my body in ways he wouldn't use his own hand for.

I named him Jesse. The baby, I mean. He breathed long enough for me to name him.

He was blue. The cord was wrapped around his neck. But that wasn't the worst of it. His arms never developed. They were tucked against his body, elbows softly out; his legs were wrapped together by skin. Nothing ever separated out. He looked like a fish.

But he was my boy. I spent hours in my mom's bathtub every day, since after I had to quit work, I couldn't afford my own place anymore. I took the hot baths the doctors said would stop the hurting. Thought I was boiling him half the time. Thought that was the reason so often babies came out red as lobsters, screaming.

I named him Jesse. His father doesn't even know he's a father.

The doctors took him away.

He was blue when he was born, like a fish, and fish don't make noise.

They thought they took him away, but they didn't. Not really. My breasts still give milk and I can feel him against me, sucking. I figure if he's part fish it's because I'm part mermaid. He gave up his legs to come to me. I don't know why I still have mine. I'm done with them now.

While he nurses, we sew my mermaid suit, him and me. It will hold my legs together so I can use them like the tail I used to have. It's heavy but that's okay because weight is different in water. We'll be safe when we go back home. No doctors can find us there, and no one will yell at us for being in the bathroom too long, and no one will yell at me to cover my breasts and tell me that I'm not nursing when I am. Jesse and me, we're going to the bottom of the sea. It's just like the movie there. Everyone sings and in the end, everybody's happy. It's just like the movie. At the bottom of the sea, we won't need anything or anybody because we'll have each other.

"My life has been a series of emergencies."   —Lana Turner

This week, I am lacking a little bit of god and so I go see my doctor.
In the same voice I ask my hairdresser to get rid of my roots, I tell her:
    Fix me. Make me better.
I have symptoms.

Which symptoms, my doctor asks.
The horrible ones: Heartbeat. Pulse. Inhalation. Exhalation.
And other ones, too. All the female ones. All the ones that go by three letters
    and end in syndrome and all the ones in between.
I have static from the elbows down and my eyes are full of bees.
My teeth have grown roots into my brain and at night, my back clenches
    into a fist.

This has happened before.
The last time, the doctor gave me drugs and told me to sleep for 24 hours solid
but I forgot how while waiting for the bus and walked back to her for
instructions.

Fix me, I tell her. Make me better.
You seem a little depressed, she says. I'm not depressed.
You seem a little depressed. I'm not depressed, I'm American.
You seem a little depressed.
So what if I'm a little depressed.

I decide maybe it's time to take drastic measures, see a rabbi, a manbo,
    a priest, a bottle of whisky,
a plastic surgeon, an advertising agency. I call my therapist and tell her I'm fine.
I call my chiropractor and tell her I'll be in tomorrow.

On my way out of the doctor's office, three homeless men are waiting for me.
They see the work of my hairdresser.
They begin to pretend they have cameras, shooting me over and over, and
    one says
You're so pretty. You must be in the movies.

How did they know. I *am* in the movies. I am Sweet Polly Purebred tied to
    the trackmarks.
I am Fay Wray at the moment King Kong's hand unfurls.
I am Frances Farmer's bathtub, Jayne Mansfield's car top,
    Marilyn Monroe's dial tone,
Linda Lovelace's tonsilitis as I walk to the pharmacist, silver screen tight in
    one hand.

I trade it for a bottle of small new gods, sweet pastel buddha bellies in an
    orange case,
or white and shining as the projection booth light from somewhere above
that makes us all move until those words, THE END.

I open wide. I say cheese. I swallow.

lather,
rinse
and
revolution

protecting jane doe
(found scrawled on advertising broadsides)

people look   everybody Look

this is a Message to the People of san francisco

Patricia Hearst says
   if you see somebody
      acting Sexual
         to Jane
            please call the Police

          Janesfather
        doesn't want any   Guys
             messing around
        with his daughter

THE BEST FRIENDS MAKE THE BEST MISTAKES

{45

        Patricia Hearst will Pay

          the first 20
             people that show up
         at the meeting

          Patricia Hearst
            is having
         a meeting

            at 6th and Market

        Patricia Hearst will be talking
                 tomorrow at 8 pm,
           10 pm and also
            12, also
                3 pm and also

     Patricia Hearst will be talking about
       the People who raped

        Jane   people raped
        Jane
                    says
        she is
                    a Rape
        Victim   Jane says guy
                            are Raping her
                    all the time

WINDOWS 2000 IS COMING

                            all the Time

                Patricia Hearst wants
            everybody who reads
            her Newspaper
        to Look
    don't touch
        everybody/ Look
    don't touch/ everybody
        don't touch Jane

46}

Patricia Hearst
doesn't want
anybody

touching Jane.

What will it be?
the waitress asks.

Past 2 in the morning
and Ethan and I are lit
by coffee and the fluorescent lights of the diner.
The waitress and her preservative hair,
her apron pink as candy hearts
brings us more coffee again,
Ethan with 2 creams 1 sugar,
mine with 1 sugar 2 creams.
He says *you realize this is it?*
and I think he means coffee but he
means the world.
You realize this is it,
the world is ending soon.

The coffee sinks my spoon, spins it down,
sucks it down towards the center of the earth
the world spins on its axis below us
as I suck my coffee down
and I am squinting at the neon DINER sign
that halos Ethan in newborn red
the N is out and the R beats on and off
in time with my heart after coffee.

The world is ending and unless you are
reborn to God when He comes for us
you will be left behind, he says,
to burn

The R in the sign has gone out.
I'm serious, he says, his hands
thin, listening animals, two by two,
jerking with his words.
The world is an egg, fragile and round, inside of
God. It is about to be reborn to him.
You can feel it coming.

I am squinting my eyes at the neon
lights and all that is left
is a large red D I E; we sit nuclear
in its glow,
Ethan's eyes aflame.

You can feel it coming, he says
the greenhouse effect   *(contraction)*
worldwide famine   *(contraction)*
this week's war   *(contraction)*
AIDS and those gays   *(contraction)*
animal cloning   *(contraction)*
high school shootings   *(contraction)*
and they're coming closer
together

apocalypse now
the mark of the beast
the horsemen are coming, now
closer and closer and stronger
and stronger and when the world ends
when the (contractions)
stop
when the
kingdom
comes
which way
will you

fall

we are immobile
ruined by neon
we sit as hopeless as morning
shaking from coffee
in the eggshell fragile
belly of God
and I don't
know what to say
when the waitress
inevitable as death

asks *will that be all*
is there anything else
will that be all
is there anything
else? She is waiting for our
money and my
answer.

messiah

the alarm goes off on his revolution

    cup of coffee, cream and revolution

reads the daily revolution:

    partly cloudy, 70% chance of revolution

        tobacco companies admit smoking causes revolution

        four killed in three-car revolution

goes to the bathroom and takes a revolution

    lather, rinse and revolution

takes the #22 revolution

    arrives 10 minutes late for the revolution

logs on to the revolution

    pushes paper around his revolution

takes a lunch revolution

    picks up dry-cleaning from the revolution

answers the ringing revolution

    stays late to finish a revolution

takes the #9 to meet friends for a revolution

    discuss their days at the revolution

drinks a frosty cold revolution

    and then a shot of revolution

        gets a little drunk on cheap revolution

hails a yellow revolution

    gets home in time for monday night revolution

pets the cat sitting on his revolution

as he eats yesterday's left-over revolution
brushes and flosses his revolution
    gets down on his knees and prays to revolution
puts his head on his revolution
    counts sheep jumping over a white picket revolution
until he falls

            fast

                asleep.

local gods for urban insomniacs

1.　　*vcr*

12:00
:
12:00
:
12:00
:

2.　　*crosswalk*

walk
don't
walk
walk
don't

3.　　*light switch*

off

on

off
on

off

Sorry for the mess.

Please feed the dog.

Jemma, do you remember listenting to the Who over and over when we were kids? Don't wanna cause no big s-s-sensation. I wanted to be Roger Daltrey but always felt more like Tommy before the pinball. I mean, I could hear and see, but I was still dumb.

Mom, you always said to try and make Dad proud.

I'm sorry to go this way. I never meant to hurt anybody. I just hurt too much all the time.

Mom, I never made Dad proud.

Please feed the dog. She never hurt nobody.

Jemma your Who record is by the bed—my g-g-g-generation   hope I die before I get old—sorry I never returned it. Mom, sorry I couldn't be who you wanted. I tried. Delia you deserve a better man than me

I tried to stop the mess with the garbage bag Hope it worked. No funeral please. All I do is make a mess. I tried to stop it. Don't remember me at all. Delia you deserved a better man than me Delia you deserved this Delia I never hurt nobody   Delia

Please feed the dog. The bills are paid through the first. I'm sorry if this hurts you but you all hurt me first and I had to Jemma I scratched your Who record now my generation skips the Who hope I die—hope I die—hope

—hope

aunt irene tells time

let's see. it happened before
uncle mel's triple bypass but
before grandpa pete fell from the
chair and broke his hip
and before your father died but
after he found the mass in his throat
and grandma elena must have been dead already
because it was in spring since
cousin jean had already
miscarried from her third pregnancy
and duffy the dog hadn't been
hit by the car yet
so it must've been
1988.

54}

california dinner party: white with flounder

(overheard)

What I hear you saying
is that it's your experience
that   undercapitalized
people   of   color
are responsible for most
of   the   problems
in   this   country.

I don't want to invalidate
what   you   feel,
but I think we can agree
to   disagree   on   this.

It's   so   good
that   you   feel
this   is   an   open
and   free   environment
in which you are safe
to   express   yourself.

{55

the jewish atheist mother has her say

baby, there is no
god but
they'll kill you
for him.

bringing up baby

"what language is it/big enough/to say your name?"   —Ntozake Shange

I read in my queer white Americanese
about your ten month pregnancy
(now, that's gotta
hurt) and I'm thinking your "baby",
how different, black or mixed race,
your baby would look next to mine,
white or mixed race

and these babies still
they will learn
to stand, walk, read,
cry and wail, those baby things
cutting their teeth on language
too late to save us
shaking their rattles
and dreaming the dreams
before language, in which
we are warm, safe and dry

and does such a place
even exist for us, when
if I say to you
I'm hungry
or *I'm tired*
what you get
is at the least
the white woman is hungry
the white woman is tired
no me/know you

mean you learn to read/to write in black
and i have had to learn to write/in white
write/myself in/between the lines

how can we ever speak
to each other

{57

how can I hear you say the *I*
before *am,* hungry, tired
and not *that black woman*
is tired/is hungry/

can we/
wail/can we/speak/we/
in any language we've
learned without
eliding, without
erasing, without saying
no, you don't get it
you don't get it
at all

in a different understanding
could we call
each other
baby
could our eyes
communicate
for real/tell us
everything we need to
get it
not that black/white
woman
and what will it take
until we can wrap
our lips around
possible
as our mother,
forgiving
nothing
forgetting
nothing
apologizing
for nothing
for these words
that mean

/everything

/understanding

/nothing

can we learn
them, wail them
loud
can we make it
this world/worth/word/
ours/all/ours?

what language
is it
big enough
to say
our names?

you break it, you bought it

Like some families all have the same last name, all his parents' restaurants have the same last name: Lac. The Ristorante du Lac, the Hotel du Lac and Cafe du Lac. All on lakes. All restaurants on lakes with gift shops. I used to think that his parents were very important to own the lakes. I only found out later that they only own the restaurants and gift shops.

It's a block away from my school, the Ristorante du Lac. Everything in there is tiny. Sometimes I stop in there on my walk home from school. I've never seen anything like it. It's like a whole museum of tiny. Tiny spoons, tiny thimbles, tiny bells, tiny glass animals, all lined up on glass shelves.

You break it, you bought it.

Jesse, the owner's son, breathes that over my shoulder when I'm in there looking at stuff. He works there, but just because they make him, the way rich people make their kids do the things they do, like work at their businesses and play golf so they can meet the right people. So they can become the right kind of people, people like their parents.

I'm not the right kind of people. My mom's never baked anything in her life or played cards in the middle of the day with other women and my dad would never play golf. When he's not working, he's watching tv.

You break it, you bought it.

His voice makes me jump, makes my hand hit the bottom of the glass swan pond. They hop up and clang back down on the glass, some of them landing on their sides. My hands stumble to set them right. He shoves my hands out of the way, makes the swans perfect again.

He knows it would take three years of Christmas for me to get one of those swans, or the glass cats, or the glass anythings that they have. He's daring me.

He doesn't get that I know that, too. I'm not really clumsy. I don't scare so easily. I always rattle the tray, but I never break anything.

Sometimes his mother breezes through, never really working, but

60}

always around, the way owners are. She always puts her hands on my shoulders from behind me, gently pushes me over to the sale rack swans, some with a wing missing, or a beak chipped off. *Aren't these* nice? she always asks. *And aren't these more in your price range? Wouldn't you like one of these?* Her thin pencil eyebrows go up on the last word of every question.

Today, right before she takes her hands off my shoulders and bobbles away to fuss at the woman working the register, she says, *You know, I haven't seen your mother since the last PTA meeting. How is she?* She doesn't wait for an answer. *Your mother must get so sick of cooking for all six of you. You all should come in here some night to eat. It'll give the dishwashing machine the night off.*

She doesn't know that *I* am the dishwashing machine. But her son knows. I know he knows by the way he walks up behind me as I move away from the sale shelf, back to the full-price swans. I can feel his breath on my neck, but he doesn't say anything. His breath is warm on my neck and I wait for him to say something but he doesn't. We stand there for a few minutes, and I realize he's not going to say anything. His mouth is so close to my neck he's almost kissing me and his hand is touching the sleeve of my coat.

That's when I realize that he wants me. Or wants the kind of thing from me that you can't ask the right kind of girl for. His mother calls him from the register and he jolts away, fast.

I reach up to the shelf, wrap my hand around the center swan, the largest one. I slip it into my pocket and walk out.

I wait until I get a block away to snap its neck, smash it into glitter under my shoe, over and over again, grind it into the pavement, dance on it until it is harmless, until it is gone forever. I lick my thumb, which bleeds the rest of the walk home, and I've never tasted anything so good.

I don't go to the store again. I broke it, but I'll never, ever buy it. Never.

This poem costs $40,000,
    which is the price of
    a Master of Fine Arts Degree
    at a private American college
    at the end of the 20th Century.

It comes to you
courtesy of Bank of America,
    now owned by NationsBanc
    and is financed at 8 1/2% interest
    annually.

This poem is out to save the world
    one word at a time
    imbue lives with
    beauty and meaning—
and let's face it, these things
    are in short supply—$40,000 seems
    a small price to pay

until you realize that $40,000 could feed
    10,025 people Happy Meals for dinner
    or buy 160,000 condoms or 2,000 blankets
    or buy 400 morning-after pills for women
    who do not have access to
    or can not afford abortion

or maybe this poem could be the salary
    of one or two staff members
    at the suicide hotline
    so that when a poet
    who is $40,000 in debt
    calls from a pay phone
    there's someone to pick up the call

at ten cents a minute long distance rates,
    that's 400,000 minutes
during which this poem could be read 133,333 times

and at today's minimum wage,
it would still not have paid for itself before taxes

and reading
and reading any poem
and reading any poem 133,333 times
could make anyone crazy

at which point
this poem
courtesy of the Bank of America
now owned by NationsBanc
will remind you
that there have traditionally been institutions
for people who write poetry
and they're not schools.
$40,000 seems a small price to pay
to stay out of one

but while there is health insurance
and life insurance and accident
insurance and disability insurance
there is no education insurance

to help us make that moment
when words glimmer us
with epiphanies and suddenly we
are surrounded by fireflies making
love on a dark night
we are the curl and hush
of the mona lisa's
smile we are the immaculate
fingers of light reaching
through stained glass

how do you put a price on any of it
and how do you stop your hands from shaking
when you write a check
which is not a poem
to the Bank of America
now owned by
NationsBanc.

the
gun
is
of
the
opposite
sex

in that town
     5 churches
4 cops
     3 historical
landmarks
2 grocery stores
1 school

the boys   drank
cases of schlitz ripped off
from   the a&p where
someone's   brother's
cousin worked
       then tore up
the blind hill driving
in the wrong lane
      with the lights
out

the catholic girls
     fucked while they
were on the rag
    so they didn't
have to
use birth control and
upset God   or   get

pregnant

like that girl
    gang-raped
behind the a&p
    renamed slut in
the fifth grade
    by the time she
got   to sixth grade
    no one knew her
name was virginia

not even   her teacher

mr. aber
          who was gay
          —no, just a
bachelor

mrs. keefer
          who drank so
much
          —no, just dizzy

and her daughter
          who had black
eyes
               —no, just clumsy

like patrick   who
lost three fingers
          to the apple cider
press
judith, killed by
          a jet skier while
swimming
and peter,   killed by
          his dad
while hunting   deer

near where
the harris family lost their
house   to   a   fire
when their heater, the
oven,   ignited

          the paper bag
               filled with dog
shit on the lawn   of
the only   black
family

          the   cops   never
came   any of the

43 times

at the scene of
        another   drunken
car wreck   on   a   blind
hill,   cops   shrugging
        kids   will   be
kids

                returning the
boys to their homes
        where the fathers
stood up   from the tv
                undid   their
belts to
        show their sons
        how to take it
        like a man

and the mothers
        gumbled upstairs
        to   pray   their
sayers

gank
        Thod
                they were
all

                shafe.

Picture this: a memory like a movie. The frame of experience. Something's burning. I have never really seen a giraffe. Stop. Focus. Let me start again, slower.

Neurology: a study of nervous. They have proved that the things we imagine are real. In a random sample, people were asked to visualize a giraffe at 5 feet, 15 feet, 500 feet. The optic nerve contracted and expanded accordingly, proving that when we think, we see. When we think we see, we are projecting our memories onto experience. Memory: a unit of measurement describing the distance between past and present. The mind takes from life, gives life back to us in Technicolor, a snapshot from a family album.

In this one I am five. I am in a pink party dress, decked out like a birthday cake in layer over layer of lace. I have a party favor in my mouth, and my eyes are swollen from crying. I do not remember why I was crying, but when you say "girl" or "lace" or "party favor" this is where I go, that image, my life.

I see it the way I see my body now, my arms below me, my legs outstretched (when I say "legs" I see Juliette Prowse in a stockings commercial: Nothing Beats a Great Pair of L'Eggs and the things we used to do with those L'Eggs eggs) and when you say "eggs," I see breakfast, smell coffee scalding and the morning that something was wrong so everything burned: breakfast, the kitchen, even tears.

When we talk about the mind we are talking about our memories, remaking the world in our own images.

There would be no science in a world I made, there would be no burning at breakfast, no coffee yells so strong the dogs cringed under the furniture. No lace dresses, no growing up, no awkward phase, no relief in memories: "Furniture": the blue velvet couch I vomited on my first drunk. "Vomit": so repulsive even my food won't stay with me. Binge and purge: either there's too much or never enough. Too many memories as ineradicable as furniture stains and as strong as coffee.

You hear these words and you are thinking something else, something from your world, a girl who is a girl you know or knew; coffee is the coffee cup left this morning; furniture is a bed; the girl who was drinking coffee in your bed this morning. The girl who wasn't me in your bed this morning. I must have done something to cause this. I must have set something on fire.

Memory: a unit of measurement describing the distance between past and present. This morning has less memories than childhood, when everything was bigger, except giraffes which are small enough to fit in the mind's eye. We can play with them like dolls, make them dance like Juliette Prowse, place blue velvet couches on their backs and ride them to somewhere the sunlight is the color crayons say it should be, where mothers have gentle hands and fathers lift you up so high, you are the tallest thing in the world. Feet astride his shoulders like bicycle pedals, you could place another, taller father in front of him, and another, taller father in front of him, and another, taller father in front of him, as far as the mind's eye can see. And with them standing there, you could climb collarbones like a ladder until you are dizzy from the height, you are taller than a giraffe but everything is gentle and when it's time to come down, there you are, caught by arms as strong and soft as breath, and memory is meaningless since all you have ever known is this, is safe.

The mind is a camera obscura; everything upside down, meaning this is all lies, or this is only possible in the mind. The mind is a camera, meaning this is a mirror trick, a trigger, a shutter. The trap door snaps shut. It's all in how you focus.

The mind, a box of photographs. My mind, the collection

of things I know but can't bear to look at or away from. I must have done something to cause this. Everything looks like something else. The collection of things that are something else: L'Eggs eggs. A collection of things that can be used for other things: Closets have doors to hide things inside. Doors have locks to keep people out. A box that is memory. A rubber eraser on a photograph doesn't work. The persistence of vision, the persistence of revision—the persistence of revision—I'm desperate here—

—at 24 frames per second, it looks like motion, this home movie of a 5-year old in a party dress, this homemade mind motion made out of stills. It looks like the picture moves, that's why we call it a movie. The motion of memory when the only thing moving is the film and a girl who wasn't me.

adolescence, that process of
dividing from the rest of the world

splitting like a cell against
parents, away from friends

the isolation of the unfamiliar body
that no longer even remembers itself

but propels upwards,
forgetful.

that year that fathers tremble over, when
daughters become that impossible thing: womanly.

forgetful, I spent a year writing poems
feverish, as if each was the first

about girls, me, and all
the things that happened to those girls, me

and all those poems, monsters the way
adolescence is monstrous

overripe and uncontrollable
like summer or tumors,

forgetful, I left
a notebook open.

my father traced my path away from him
through my words, the path I wrote.

the doctor towered in front of me,
a man in command

of the way cells
divide upon themselves

watching puberty invade his daughter like a disease
the wild, unchecked growth, the enemy

a 14-year old host vulnerable to foreign bodies
the enemy, the trembling, the bodies

the notebook in his hand
with the words about girls, me, and all

the poems that happened
to a girl, me and all

he said:
"you know who

that girl is,
don't you?

that girl's
a whore."

Touch your toes.

Satan Says touch your toes.

Satan Says pat your head.

Satan Says pull your ear Satan Says touch your chin Satan Says rub your belly lick your lips Hey—

Satan didn't Say

to lick your lips.

Satan Says fill the ice tray.

Satan Says turn the radio up.

Satan Says shave your legs.   {75

Satan Says pluck your eyebrows Satan Says touch yourself Satan says smoke a cigarette Satan Says writhe Satan Says have a drink.

He's not coming.

Satan didn't Say

he's not

coming.

Satan Says pour a drink Satan Says have another. Satan Says have another. Satan Says there's some coke in your coat. Satan says cut a line. Satan Says cut another. Satan Says too much.

Just

kidding.

Satan Says cut another. Satan Says touch yourself. You've got jitters.
Your hands aren't steady. Keep it cool. Satan says have a drink Satan says
have a cigarette Satan Says he's married Satan says better than nothing
Satan Says he's not coming check the time.

Satan didn't

say that's the   Doorbell sAtan sAys that's enougH   satan   says Love Thy
Neighbor   satan Says kind of   Sloppy Satan   says he   Wants
        you satan says   He's   not
        Coming   Satan Says walk   straight satan says   having Fun yet?
satan says you've got   to Be Kidding satan   says   You made
yoUr   Bed   satan saYs cHeck   the tiMe   thAt's   the
        doUrbellE

N   N   NNnno w. Whut   re   U   gong   to du?e

you never forget your first

out of town boy   junior high school party   just 14   vodka drinks
things i don't   remember   vodka drinks   english beat   *she said will*
you remember

said i'll never forget you   the next day   in the hall   at school   you
told me   you were a state-ranked hurdler   you told everyone i was easy
never saw you again

you left me   a secret   ripped stockings   passed out   bloody legs
vomiting in a pink bathtub   your name   bruises

you hugged me   in the hall   you told everyone   i was easy   i'd rather
be easy   than raped

i came to   with no clothes   no clothes were thick enough   wearing
shame for underwear   i shoved the bloody stockings   into the bathroom
trash

apologized to the host   for messing up   the bathroom   and left
you were   already gone

i pushed   at the bruises   trying to remember   your touch

once the hangover   and internal injuries   were healed   i had nothing
to remember   my first time with   except sex

i bruised my way   through thousands of fucks   snake charming men   out
of their pants   looking for another rapist like you   so i could do it again
so i could do it better

found another one   he led me   by the hand   into a dark room   at a
party   i punched him in the throat   and got away   he wasn't you

the bruises you left   bone-deep fossils of your desire   it's better   to be
irresistable   than raped

if you hadn't   wanted me so badly   you would have done it   so gentle like
candlelight   i know it   i know if you   hadn't needed me so   violently

you could have waited until   i wasn't passed out

you could have   given me   rose-sweet kisses   i could have been your
preteen penthouse playmate   i would have said yes   but you never asked
and i couldn't speak

do you ever   think of me   the way i think of you   was that your   first
time   too   you never forget   your first   rapist

it's been 15 years   i never touched you   when you hugged me   in the hall
at school   you were with another girl   did you like her better?   never saw
you again

come back   so i can say yes   this time   do it again   now that i know
what to call   what you did

this time i'll be ready   i like it rough now   and i'm done with romance   i
never met another man   who loved me so much   at first sight   he had to
hurt me   to do it

50, 49:

I count back-
wards at night,
some thread, some stitches
in time, something I lost,
bus fare, a hole in my pocket

as I unreel the day behind me
waiting for sleep like
a bus, a guest, a gift, a guess
a first date, a last fight
the movie screen last night
where the hero
never
wore white:

50, 49.
The hypnotherapist tells me
to think of somewhere safe.

46, 45, 44.
I count backwards from ten.
I can't think of anywhere.
I pay the man his money.

46, 45, 44.
I count backwards from ten.

46, 45, 44.
I count backwards from ten.

46, 45, 44.
I count backwards from ten,
unreal, the day behind me
and so I'm waiting for the bus
and this guy says to me,
why don't you tie me to your kitchen table

and stomp on me with those big boots?

36, 24, 36.
Paper towels.
Laundry detergent.
Light bulbs.

22, 21, 20.
Never stare at a light
while lying on your back.
You'll go blind.

19, 18, 17.
they say it will smell like bubblegum
they say count backwards from ten
they say breathe deep
they say it will be over when I wake up
they say it won't leave a scar
they say breathe deep
they say

16, 15, 14.
I count backwards from ten.

16, 15, 14.
these big boots

13, 12, 11.
walking somewhere safe

10, 9.
suntanned from light bulbs

8, 7.
going blind.

6, 5.
the bus never comes

5
bubblegum

4
light

3
movie

2
night

1.

1.

1.

anti-nowhere league

for Bucky Sinister

nature gave
bright colors
spikes, spurs
and loud noises

to its endangered ones,
its helpless pretties,
to keep them safe
but nature

forgot us,
the casualties of adolescence
who inherited a cold
war   a race war

a class war   a sexual
revolution   a battle of the sexes   an energy
crisis and one question:
why are you so hostile?

we ransacked our childhoods
to armor ourselves:
stole the ivory soap that could not
keep us clean, stole the elmer's

glue that held neither
our school projects
nor our families
together

used it
to bully our hair up
into arrowheads,
hypodermic tips,

barbed wire fences
and buzz saw blades;

and went to see the Ramones.
we circled around each other

tight and low
as toxic as possible
to discourage predators
from attacking

while the band's three-chord crunch
did everything that parents,
schools and churches
could not.

when they yelled
GABBA GABBA HEY   WE ACCEPT YOU   WE ACCEPT YOU
we threw our molotov cocktail bodies
after the sound

from a six-foot stage.
the air, the adrenaline
sang in our veins that
since bruises are nothing new,

there are only new bruises
and we waited for
the only impact
we knew how to make

but for the first time
GABBA GABBA HEY
hands

caught us

dragged us

from

the nothing
of the air

flipped the bird
to gravity

soared us over
the garden of heads
that thrashed like flowers
in a storm

gave a *fuck*
you to natural
law as we sailed

legs
over heads
GABBA GABBA HEY
over asses
over elbows

split our lips
tore our clothes
stole our boots but
those hands

WE ACCEPT YOU

did not
let us
fall.

1.   Nothing chooses us.

2.   Mute, we talk in pictures,
glyphs for what's
inside the bodycave

3.   Claud is at the tattoo
parlor again
today; ink drives bands
of barbed wire
or flame or killer
bees into
his body,
wrists, ankles,
and throat.

"I have a problem
with boundaries,"
he says.

The world gets
under his skin.

It's a
rush.

4.   These words choose us.
We put them in our mouths,
feed our skins.
We are hungry.

Anna's wrist
has *integrity*

Roger's shoulder
holds a *priceless*
spear.

On Veronica's back

flames of
liquid
fire;

the POEM inside
of Bucky's lower lip.

D.S.'s forearms know
it's a girl/it's a boy/

sucker

and one bicep is
NOT CRAZY

Claud's arm is
HIV+
two inches
high, blood
red.

Already out-
side, we slipped
a needle under
our skins and closed
the door
behind us.

5.   We take our clothes
off but language
never
leaves us
alone.

6.   We are now
somewhere
else. It's
warmer.

Claud wears
his sleeves
rolled up.

a guide to kissing in public for lesbians*

this is a matter
of life and
death.

know the warning signs:
uncomfortable
pressure, fullness,
squeezing
or even pain
in the chest
is a pulse
a pressure
in your chest
a matter of life
and death
that lasts
for more
than a few
minutes.

here are the actions
for survival:

recognize the signals
around you

stop

whatever
you're doing

open the airway
gently
lift her chin
towards you
with one hand

---

* Instructions taken from the American Heart Association's
Guide to CPR for Adults

you want to tilt
her head
back

you want
to breathe

pulse

gently

open

lean over
put your ear

close

to her mouth

look
at her chest
for a moment

her chest
rising

this is a matter
of life

her breath
listen

feel
for it
on your cheek

keep your hand
under her chin
lifting up
gently
up

make an air-
tight seal
your mouths

for more

a few minutes

immediately
give

breath

take

pulse

your hand

pulse

find her

mouth

air-tight

find her

mouth

pulse

lifting up

slide

her chin

your fingers

down

feel

(but know the warn/ing
signs

beat/ing

beat/ing)

That day, that day we had our first real date, if real is the name you give to someone you can suddenly give a subcutaneous smile, if real is what I called the frightening urge to introduce you to my mother, if real is the only name I can give to the last night that I saw you before that day, your body, my mouth, your mouth gasping, "nobody's ever done that before," my smartass reply that oh, people have done that before; your release to me, the first you'd ever had, the only one you'd ever given away.

We went to the beach, kissed as awkwardly as seagulls, afraid that we could speak in tongues, afraid our desire was so palpable we wore it like neon sunscreen, afraid that we'd look like what we were: lovers, and not what we were: girls, our bikinis just barely covering our shame and desire and we stayed at the beach until dark that day, watching the water swell and roll, ashamed and titillated by what would come next, ashamed and afraid for wanting it, afraid it might not happen at all.

We took the train back to the city, looking, both of us, straight ahead, not discussing where we would go, indicted somehow by our houses' proximity to each other.

The train spilled us out into the dark, salt-sticky and nervous with night. The last time we shared in the dark huddled between our skins and our clothes, filled our mouths until we could barely speak, followed us like an unwelcome third.

I offered to walk her home. Not take her home, not go home with her. And so we walked. The night tripped us slowly along, like small waves underfoot, pulling us.

A small fleet of young men scrambled in the street a block ahead, shoving and pushing against each other, rough and loud as surf.

She sighed, tired, and used to boys and so unused to me, she slid her arm around my waist and tucked her head between my ear and my shoulder. I smelled her salt, her sweat.

The young men approached, larger and louder than they had seemed, weaving like boxers, agitated and unafraid, looking for provocation, for something to test their tentative manhood, inscribe their brotherhood.

She had tucked her head between my ear and my shoulder. I sucked in my breath, so close to the danger of the dark, so close to her house, so close to close to her. I sucked in my breath, the overgrown boys barely half a block away. I put my eyes low, my head tucked down, pushed our bodies forward like the tide. Her nose sank against my neck as I braced from the impact, prepared for the impact.

She sank her nose in my neck. I smelled her salt. I ducked my head and held my breath, gripped her like a life preserver.

The boys rushed towards us like high tide. Let it happen, my head said.

We were two blocks from her house.

Whatever's coming, let it happen.

(for Stuart Matis, 33, who ended his life
on the steps of the Santa Clara Church of Latter Day Saints
when he could no longer reconcile
his faith and his sexuality)

This is not a love story
of a forbidden coupling.

The gun
is of the opposite
sex.

The state sanctions
their union,
gives them license,
pronounces them
man and gun, how the West
was won, that old
American dream.

They live together
in California for a short
time.

The gun makes his hands
manly but his bones feel
so giddy, girlishly soft. He rests
his head on the gun's narrow
shoulders. The gun
is strong and silent.

It takes two hands
to pray, to shoot
and to type.

The man writes his own vows:
I am now free.
I am no longer
in pain and I no

{93

longer hate
myself. As it turns
out, God never intended
for me to be straight...
shooter, laughs the gun. Straight shooter. Get it?

Her mouth is hard and round.
Their union is sin.

Together they go to the
   Church
Say Temple, says the gun.
Your temple.
   Church has no idea
   that as I type this letter

The gun checks his spelling.
Write about me, she says.

   there are surely boys and girls

and guns, says the gun

   on their calloused knees
   imploring God
   to free them...

God doesn't care, says the gun.
Write about me.

   ...they retire to bed
   with their finger
   pointed to their head
   in the form of a gun.

Thank you, says the gun.
The honey moon sets
on their wedding morning.

He has waited a lifetime
for her, every night
practicing with his fingers

to his head

on the steps of the church
the gun jabbers
Do you take me
take me now

The rest is under
investigation;
a few shattered teeth,
a note and three gallons
of blood. The police claim
a bullet entered through
his soft palate, ripping through
the muddy tissue of the brain
fracturing the skull
and leaving a powder burn
ring

the church denies any involvement
but the fingerprints
of latter-day saints were found
all over the scene.

The widow gun
was led away
in police custody
her hard, round mouth
muttering
the other temple
it was supposed to be
the Mormon temple

My baby keeps her hair
short.
Number 2 guard, 1/4 inch white oster clippers short
short hair.

Not I'm-depressed-and-I'm-going-to-shave-my-head short,
just short.

She's got beautiful baby-short hair.
Baby short, not basketball-player short
or concentration camp short or
or military short or militant short;
not monk short
or cancer short.
Just
short.

Her gray hairs shine like
flashbulb filaments,
one for each brilliant
idea she has.

She's getting more and more
gray. She says it's my
fault.

My baby keeps her hair
short:
Nothing to cling to desperately,
nothing to get tangled up in.
My baby keeps her hair short—
she likes it that way
and so
do I.

my
mouth
is
a
wound
and
you
want
to
kiss
me

My fire-eating career came to an end
when I could no longer tell
when to spit and when

to swallow.
Last night in Amsterdam,
1,000 tulips burned to death.

I have an alibi. When I walked by
your garden, your hand
grenades were in bloom.

You caught me playing
loves me, loves me
not, metal pins between my teeth.

I forget the difference
between seduction
and arson,

ignition and cognition. I am a girl
with incendiary
vices and you have a filthy never

mind. If you say no, twice,
it's a four-letter word.
You are so dirty, people have planted

flowers on you: Heliotropes. Sun-
flowers. You'll take
anything. *Loves me,*

loves me not.
I want to bend you over
and whisper: "potting soil," "fresh

cut." When you made
the urgent fists of peonies
a proposition, I stole a pair of botanists'

hands. Green. Confident. All thumbs.
I look sharp in garden
shears and it rained spring

all night. 1,000 tulips
burned to death
in Amsterdam.

We didn't hear the sirens.
All night, you held my alibis
so softly, like taboos

already broken.

inductance

This week
in live current
events: your eyes.

All power can be
dangerous:
Direct

or alternating,
you, socket to me.
Plugged in and the grid

is humming,
this electricity,
molecule-deep desire:

particular friction, a charge
strong enough to stop
a heart

or start it
again; volt, re/volt—
I shudder, I stutter, I start

to life. I've got my ion
you, copper-top,
so watch how you

conduct yourself.
Here's today's
newsflash: a battery of rolling

blackouts in California, sudden,
like lightning kisses:
sudden, whitehot

darkness and you're
here, fumbling for

that small switch

with an urgent surge
strong enough to kill
lesser machines.

Static makes hair raise,
makes things cling,
makes things rise like

a gathering storm
charging outside
our darkened house

and here I am:
tempest, pouring out
mouthfulls

of tsunami on the ground,
I've got that rain-soaked kite,
that drenched key.

You know what it's for,
circuit-breaker, you know
how to kiss until it's hertz.

kissing with the lights on

You told me you like my mouth.
You want to kiss me.

My mouth is a wound and you
want to kiss me.

But you're like
that: You want to go
leaping over cliffs—
you want to go
drinking poison
and then write pretty poems about it—
and all I want to do is
fuck you.

You want flowers and sonnets and us
to be together until the end of the world and I'd
just like a blow job. I'd just like
to see your face when you come. I'd just like
to be friends.
that's what I'd really like.
Something warm and snuggly like a friendship.
and to fuck you.

The flowers are going to die and the cliffs are
going to erode and we might as well go fuck
since we're going to anyway.
We'll fuck and fight and eat and drink and smoke and fuck and smoke and fuck and
get married

And six months from now
we'll stop making the world stop
to fuck each other

and one year from now
I'll get fat and you'll go bald and
I'll take prozac and you'll take viagra
I'll get obsessed with my biological clock

and my career
and you'll get obsessed with your hairline
and your career

and two years from now
you'd rather watch reruns than fuck me
and I'd rather be drinking than fuck you
so we'll drink in separate bars and one night
someone who likes my mouth will buy me a drink
that drink will be attached to a hand
there will be a human holding that drink
the kind with ears

and I will tell whoever it is
all about you
and how we used to forget to eat when we were in bed for three days
and your ears will be burning across town
where you are telling whoever it is how I don't understand you

and two years from now, that girl with that drink
she will nod that yes that I am nodding at you tonight
that nod, that yes that means you're not coming home
because just for a second the world has gone away
because just for a second there's someone who understands you

and that night it will be her pretty mouth you want
and that night I will pass out at home, alone
with a bottle that reminds me of us
because it'll be empty
because it'll be gone
I will pass out waiting for you
to come
home
listening to country music—and I hate
country music—
but I'll be feeling tragic
it'll be the most romantic moment
I've ever had and
I'll be alone

and you'll be across town
with that girl who right now is in high school

and right now I just met you
and right now I think you should take me home and fuck me
because it only gets uglier from here
we only get uglier from here
so take me to the edge of that cliff you love
and pour me a shot of your silky poison
you can take this mouth
this wound you want
but you can't kiss
and make it
better.

You want a place in my heart
but it's already full.

You're needy
but I'm generous,
so I found somewhere else
for you to stay.

You can lodge in my
appendix, that organ
that names the part
of the book
that no one reads.

Everyone fingers
the spine,
peruses the foot
notes but no one
reads the
appendix.

We live in a culture
of heroes, of muscle.
No one likes
the appendix,
the guy who quietly
takes shit
day after day
just to stick
around.

There's only so much any of us can
take. The appendix can't take
being ignored. Inflamed by self-
importance, the appendix will swell
until it is so full of shit
it explodes like popcorn.

You want a place in my heart, but it's already
full. There's not much to recommend the
appendix, but it's all I can offer
you, along with
this advice:

It's hard to love someone who's
full of shit.

It's hard to love something
that's only important
when it makes trouble.

Don't rock a boat
that doesn't need you
on board.

There's only so much
any of us can take.

Take or leave the appendix,
but remember this: Behave
or I'll cut you out.

My girlfriend would prefer
that I not fuck you.

That's what she said.

I love a woman who speaks
her mind and most of all I love
her.

In the interest of keeping
my promise,
I will just lie here and let you
do all the work.

I gave you the ampersand
of my heart.
What did you give me?
a goddamn etc.

Seduction isn't
what it used to be. These days,
I translate your French kisses.
You don't even notice
my embellishments.

No one speaks the universal anguish
of love anymore. Cherubs pack heat.
They no longer use quivers—
anything that trembles
is a natural disaster.

We live in California,
where subduction leads to orogeny—
it's science, you say;
something wet and dense sinks
under something lighter.

In Arizona, they are waiting
for beachfront property. It's inevitable—
sooner or later
we break
along faultlines.

When I tell you I'm scared,
you say, "Learn to swim"
before sleep pulls you away from me.
I roll over and over, restless tide
in your swimming pool sheets,

some shallow end for us.
Nothing can live
in the sterile clean of chlorine
and this, after all the lies I've learned,
this sinking

feeling: spinning at the whim
of whitecapped deaths and endings.

We'll have to find something else. These sheets
are too pale for us. Angels aren't white at all,
and neither are ghosts.

My sweet   217 dead in plane crash
O! As the heart beats and is   decapitated in mass graves
the mystery of you   executed for stealing state secrets
by and by   a cyclone's wake
love leaping like   1.5 million homeless in India
a deep stream, a   massive power outage
vision of angels   crash with inbound subway
the stars   attempted murder
rushing to greet you, my   charge of animal cruelty
so beloved   kidney sold to debt collector
But O heart!   attack
heart!   arrest
heart!   broke   O
sweet everything O all
your sweet nothings
and how heart!   how
baby   the hell please
how baby did this
heart!   O   how
the hell
did this
happen

what I am asking you for when I ask you for breakfast

To say the place, Albuquerque,
your mouth must do three things:
sigh, kiss, then almost smile.

I ask you for breakfast
something to fill the mouth
when what I want to ask
you for is something else
for my tongue to do:

a new word to wrap around

and it is not in me
this morning
when what I need
is coffee
and what I am
supposed to do
is say goodbye
to Albuquerque
to you

to four days built of words
and breath
to four days of the living bodies that hold them
to the words living for you in my body

Albuquerque, a word that is not made of
English, my tongue,
so I will borrow someone else's to give to you
with coffee:

a *shalom*, an *aloha*
any way of saying departure
that is also a greeting

this is a word that I want to give you over coffee
a word in Albuquerque,

the sigh, the kiss, and the smile

a word that means I will see you again,
that there is something I want
when coffee is done.

It started that night, that night when you asked, "Would you love me if I got my hair cut?"

I said, *You're beautiful no matter what.*

And you smiled. You always had a beautiful smile.

You went to sleep in my arms and the next day came back with a very fashionable—though extreme—haircut.

And you said, "Do you still love me?"

And I said, *Of course I do.*

You looked beautiful and you smiled your beautiful smile only a little smaller and you asked "Would you love me if I was bald?"

And I said, *Of course—bald is something time does to men and bald is how nature begins babies and we're all bald under our hair and anyway you're beautiful and I love you.*

And you smiled your beautiful smile and fell asleep in my arms.

The next night as I licked your beautiful, naked head, you asked, "Would you love me if I had no ears?"

And I said, *Of course—ears are only good for hanging earrings on and holding glasses up; unless they're our joke* and I made my fingers into bunny ears and you hopped sideways in the bed.

I told you: *What's important is inside,* and your smile turned up like a hook with something caught on the end of it.

Your smile sharpened like a key into a knife.

You smiled in your sleep all night long and it was still a beautiful smile.

Thankfully, you still had ears when you came home the next day, but that was the day you began taking parts of you away anyway. You took me seriously about the importance of the inside, and you took them away, the insides.

Our jokes went first—I made my bunny ears and you didn't hop.

Then our memories—I'd remind you of our jokes and you'd smile your beautiful smile and just say "Oh."

"I don't remember."

Then your habits, your hours, your appearance, your clothing.

Finally, you changed your address, smiling your beautiful smile.

I put my bunny ear fingers behind my head, told you *I love you, no matter what. Remember, it's what's on the inside that counts.*

You said, "What insides?" and "I don't remember."

Then you walked out.

Since everything changed but your smile, I go looking for your smile every night, on other faces, with other names. Whispering what was your name into what I hope is your mouth, I pry my fingers into mouth after mouth, body after body, whispering *Are you in there?*

I find glimpses of you here and there, shards of your smile, and I kiss all of them, love all of them, I collect them up like small broken things, waiting to gather them all together and bring you back. I hold these fragments close to me every night, and I whisper to them.

I remember. And I'll always love you. No matter what.

bedhead
for Eirean Bradley

some of us are loved
even though we're the last
to believe it,
we are loved
quietly, it is impossible—
believing that   we are
loved   even though
we wear   the evidence
and cannot   get rid   of it
the way others do; most days

send us reeling
back,
our hearts,   strong,   stupid   huskies,
dragging the dog sleds
of our bodies
back into bed   no matter
what is in the sky   or what
waits for us
we burrow under   the covers,
chilled   animals,
turtles with   soft shells.
it is   simple   as instinct,
simpler   than love,

as sheets wrap us   up in their   soft
arms   repair us
from the world which   we cannot
believe   might just love us enough.
we wear the evidence   all day

scrubbing and
soaking and
still
the tumbleweed hair
water can't get rid of
hats barely cover

comb teeth
            chew at us   the way
                                the world rips at
                                our parchment
                                skins
            not seasoned enough
    to keep us   warm,

    when it's so easy,   the confusion of love
                                and sex, bed
                    and bedhead
                        messing up your hair
    until it is a hundred   thousand   strong
                                        blind arms
                                        reaching
                                        back
                            to home,
                        eden, nirvana,
    whatever name we give
                    to that warm   place
        we need   to believe   in
                but rarely
                        reach

    in waking,
            more often   in sleep:
    the tumble dry   kisses
                in percale   solids, stripes and floral
                    bouquets.

it's impossible to talk at night

We set out our stories like fishing line and hope
something catches. Something catches fire. We
are setting small fires between our thighs. Tiny as
matchheads and warm like mother, we flicker our
fingers, ashamed or delighted. We are ashamed
and delighted with our new toys and wait for
nightfall, night falls and gravity still works so we
can see each other or not—small moving flashes,
we look for the flashes quick as fireflies then gone,
from a distance we are christmas lights, we are
stars, from further away we don't exist at all. In
this deep space, you need two points to navigate
by. There is no telling distance, 5 feet far or
50,000 miles close. It looks the same. The best
you can do is approximate. One fire is the same as
another. Fuel, ignition, oxygen, flame, then car-
bon. We sift through memory's ash; this is age,
cutting off histories like tree limbs and looking for
the rings. Something small sings: We pick flow-
ers, hold them like bells, shake them and listen.
Ripped from their stalks, we can almost hear them
dying, we can almost hear their scent. We listen
for each other, a breath, a rustle, never one point
but two, navigate through distance to each other,
navigate to where there is no need for this telling.

you have 1 new message, sent today at 12:43 a.m.

:

:

:   uh... oh. i guess that was the beep.

okay,   um... listen — i just found your number   on a scrap
of paper   on the floor   in my wallet   in the phone book
on the bathroom wall   okay, look   —   i'm actually just
dialing numbers at random but listen —

i'm   just   wondering   who you are   how you've been
what you've been up to   if you're lonely   and why
does   just the thought of you make   my lips and tongue
triple in size and   make me   hold the phone receiver
like it's some part   of you

and was that you   in my dream   on the bus   on the
radio   in the bank   across the room   in my pants
last night?

hello?   are you there?

i'm calling from chicago   dallas   new york
fayetteville   san francisco   minneapolis   sometimes
you seem   so   close

and i   keep   missing you   i miss you and i just called
tonight because i realized   i never told you

i'm dying   i mean we all are, right?   but i'm really
scared to die   alone   and i was wondering if you might
be, too   i'm scared of the dark   and i thought maybe   if
you were   too   we could sit in the dark   together
and not die yet   and maybe not   be so scared

um, okay.   i should go.   anyway, i think of you   every day   and i really hope   everything is going well   and okay.   um...   give me a call   soon.   just pick up the phone   and dial any number.   i'll be there.

bye.

I meet him in his Hawaiian shirt, his legs alabaster, his paunch and bloat, his Polaroid dangling like genitalia and he says he's been looking for me all his life.

He has saved up a lifetime of moments and pennies to come here, to see me, so that we can be together.

He snaps his shutter over and over, the stuttering flash leaving me speechless. *Yeah baby,* he says. *Just like that. Give it to me, yeah baby. Mmm so tall mmm so white yeah baby you're even—*

I shove my hand in his camera and hold him by the lens. The straps jerk in my hand. "Look at me," I tell him. "I'm tall and white, all right, but I am not the Washington Monument."

I point out my breasts, my teeth, my legs. His camera straps shrivel in my hand.

He jerks away and says it's not true, it can't be true. He covers his eyes with his hands when I try to show him the Polaroids he took of me, and finally I peel his fingers from his face like squid and push the photos against his nose.

He turns them on their sides, their heads, their sides and upright again, squinting at them nearer and farther. His squints dissolve into tears, one for each of the pennies he has saved over this lifetime, one for each of the mistaken moments he spent dreaming of me.

I am ankle-deep in his soggy regret when something in me dissolves. I look at his photographs, remember how he called me *baby,* think of how my whole life I've been too tall, called *stretch, beanpole;* how I've never been enough, somehow; never, ever a product of America, with its pilgrims, flags and fireworks. Some get wild west, I got smallpox. Some get purple mountains' majesty, I got bombs bursting in air. Some get liberty and justice for all; I got tired, hungry and poor.

But now, he sees me not as I am but as I always wanted to believe I could be. This attention, this adoration, is something I have always longed for, something I have always wanted to belong to. He has seen it in me and he has made it mine.

I feel the weight of all his pennies lifted from my shoulders. I look at the photographs and I see I am tall and slender and perhaps for him that is enough. Perhaps that's all he wants. I wipe his face with my white marble. My heart has turned to stone. I am built. I am stacked, more angular than ever before. We stand together, the U.S. standing simply for "us," and we glow as I lift his camera and he snaps photo after photo of me.

Suddenly, I am a monument to love.

And he, he is my tourist.

It kills me, the way the world is.

Literally.

I sat down to write about it, about how
every 15 seconds a woman is battered in the United States
about how a woman is raped every 1.3 minutes, about how
1 in 8 women develops breast cancer
and what I wrote was
I like you.

This is a problem. The world already has
too many of those. *I* already have too many
of those.

I sat down to write about how
desire and hate killed Matthew Sheppard

and when I write *desire*
I think of you
I *like* you
my pen sprouts snuggly kittens and spring flowers and
I hate myself for it

I like you so much I had to have
therapy for it
and
I like you so much
I fucked other people
to get rid of it
and the weekend you went to disneyland
I tried to grow mouse ears
I tried to be your e-ticket
I tried to grow up to be your
        full-service hotel except
        I won't throw you out for
        using bad words like they do
so if you say
        oh shit

oh fuck me
oh god
oh take me
I'll take you back to bed

I like you so much this
isn't in my agenda; I like you so much but this
should be a poem about breast cancer
and I like you so much this
should be a poem about genocide
and I like you so much this
should be a poem about ending capitalism
       smashing the state
       stating the obvious
       getting smashed
to tell you
       I'll fuck capitalism and patriarchy and totalitarianism
to get next to you
I will deep throat my politics
I will get more therapy that I won't need if you're near me
because therapy and politics are all about
making the world a little more perfect
when I close the door and it's you and me
the world is a little more perfect
whenever you smile at me
in a world that doesn't offer many smiles
the world is a little more perfect
the world is perfect
whenever
I'm with you.

Printed in the United States
By Bookmasters